The HEALING HEROES Book

Place a Special Photo Here

Braving the Changes When Someone You Love Is Wounded in Service

by Ellen Sabin

and _____

WRITE YOUR NAME HERE

WATERING CAN® PRESS
www.wateringcanpress.com

Author's "thank-yous"

I am grateful to the many people who supported me in this project. I'd like to particularly thank:

- David W. Sutherland (U.S. Army) for his inspiring commitment to wounded warriors and unfailing support of this project.

- David A. Williamson, MD (Neuropsychiatrist and Medical Director Inpatient Traumatic Brain Injury Program, Walter Reed National Military Medical Center); Evan M. Renz, MD (Director, U.S. Army Burn Center); and Stephen J. Cozza, MD (Professor of Psychiatry, Associate Director, Center for the Study of Traumatic Stress, Uniformed Services University) for generously sharing their time, input, and expertise.

- Vice Admiral Matthew Nathan (Surgeon General of the Navy), Tammy Nathan (U.S. Navy), and Lee Woodruff for championing this book and connecting me with invaluable experts and institutions for my research.

- And especially the many military families living with wounds from service who graciously shared their experiences and stories with me.

WATERING CAN®

When you care about things and nurture them,
they will grow healthy, strong, and happy, and in turn,
they will make the world a better place.

Growing Kids with Character

All Watering Can Press titles are available at special quantity discounts for bulk purchases for sales promotion, premiums, fund-raising, educational, or institutional use.

Watering Can Press offers customized versions of this book and will adjust content for use by nonprofits and corporations in support of their community outreach and marketing goals.

To inquire about bulk discounts or to learn more about customized book runs, please visit our Web site or e-mail info@wateringcanpress.com.

Text and illustrations © 2012 by Ellen Sabin
WATERING CAN is a registered trademark of Ellen Sabin.
Watering Can, New York, NY 10011. Printed in China in December 2012

Written by Ellen Sabin • Illustrated by Kerren Barbas • Designed by Patty Harris
ISBN: 978-0-9826416-0-6

Web site address: www.wateringcanpress.com

Dear _____ ,

It can be very hard and confusing when someone you love is wounded in military service.

You may have many questions and feel many different things. Talking about your feelings, asking questions, and learning more about that person's wounds can help you feel better.

The **HEALING HEROES BOOK** gives you a place to write about those feelings, questions, and thoughts.

When one person in a family is hurt, it affects everyone. You can use this book to help you better understand the changes that are happening around you. It will also give you ideas about how to feel better when you are down.

I am giving you this book because you are a hero and you are very special to me!

From, _____

- This book is dedicated to my father, Stanley Sabin, the kindest man I've ever known. He was a veteran who spent his life caring for people and his retirement volunteering to provide medical care to those who served our country.

- I'm honored to donate a portion of the proceeds from this book to support wounded service members and their families.

— *Ellen Sabin*

A NOTE FROM THE ARMED FORCES FOUNDATION (AFF)

The AFF is a nonprofit organization dedicated to serving military families. Through our programs, we've seen the enormous challenges faced by wounded service members and their spouses. We've also recognized the "ripple effect" of these traumas and the resulting life changes faced by military children. We asked Ellen Sabin to write this book because we believe that children deserve our support and we knew this book would fill a very important need. The AFF hopes that you find value in this book; not only for the children you love, but for yourself, as well.

A NOTE TO ADULTS

We know that dealing with the injury of a loved one is difficult for everyone.
It is especially hard for children.

When children are faced with change, they can be confused and overwhelmed.

The Healing Heroes Book helps children cope with this challenge by encouraging them to identify their questions, explore their feelings, confront their concerns, and learn healthy coping skills.

Adults can help children use THE HEALING HEROES BOOK
to help children grow through this challenge.

Be mindful and responsive to the questions children ask—your openness will help them heal.

Even if children have the skills to read this book independently,
they will likely benefit most if you read through the book with them.

Adults can also call upon the assistance of therapists or other professionals for children or members of their families to further facilitate understanding, communication, healthy coping, and healing.

- **Please note that a free Parent's Guide is available at www.wateringcanpress.com.**
This guide includes additional suggestions for supporting children through this challenge.

Table of Contents

> **A lot of things can happen when someone you love returns home from service with a wound.**

- That person may go to the hospital or need a lot of time with doctors or other health care workers to help him or her feel better.

- Other adults in your life may be really busy taking care of the person who was wounded and have less time to spend with you.

- There may be a lot of changes in your life, and that can feel confusing.

- Your other family members will also be facing changes and may be upset.

- You may have many different feelings or emotions.

This book is for you.

It will help you think about how you feel and give you a place to express those feelings.

It will give you information so you can better understand what happened to the person you love.

It will give you a chance to think about your family and all of the ways you can work as a team to support one another through the changes that are happening in your lives.

It will offer you a place to write down your questions and concerns about changes, wounds, recovery, and anything else that is important to you.

It will help you find things to do that will make you feel a little better when you are upset.

The HEALING HEROES

You are part of a military family.

Military families are special in many ways. Together they support one another and serve our country. That makes each person in your family a HERO.

When one person in a family gets hurt or wounded, it affects everyone in the family. This happens because the injury brings about change.

You, your parents, and other family members will all go through a HEALING process as you grow through the changes.

To do this, you will need to be BRAVE.

That makes you, your wounded warrior, and your other family members THE HEALING HEROES.

Note: This book is for all kids who know and love someone who has been wounded in service. That person may be their dad or mom. Other times it may be their brother, sister, or another member of their family. To keep it simple, we are going to call that person your "wounded warrior."

Remember:

This is YOUR book, and you can use it however YOU want!

You can write in it, draw pictures, keep a journal,
and collect your thoughts.

- Sometimes you may be thinking about your feelings and the changes that are happening in your life. At those times, using this book might make you feel better.

  Other times, you might want to put your book down and think about something else or do other things.

- You can do as much or as little of the book as you feel like doing. You might want to look through the whole book or you might want to skip around and just do some parts. You can also put it away and take it out again in a few days, weeks, or months from now.

- You can use this book on your own or you can share it with family, friends, teachers, or other special people in your life.

So, take your time and use your
HEALING HEROES BOOK when and how you want!

Honoring the HEROES in Your Family

Military families are special.

You are part of a very special family.

Someone in your family decided to join the military. Whether that person is a soldier, sailor, airman, or marine, they are called a "service member" because they serve our country.

That means that it's their job to protect our country, defend our freedom, and support people around the world who need help.

To do these things, your family member needs to be strong, dedicated, and brave. These are just some of the qualities that make that person a hero!

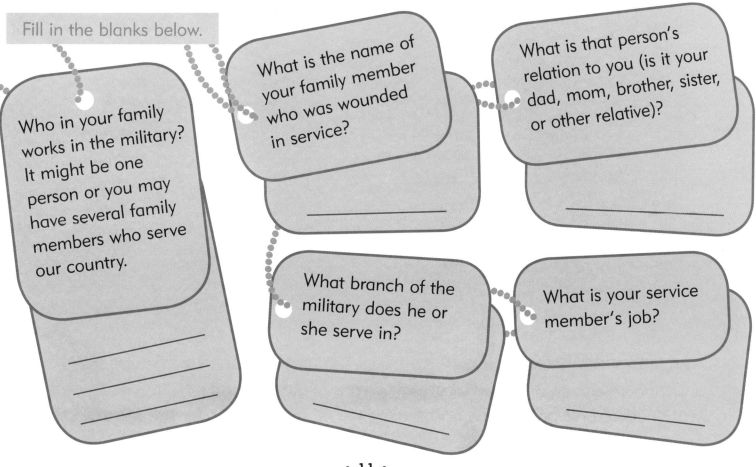

Fill in the blanks below.

Who in your family works in the military? It might be one person or you may have several family members who serve our country.

_____
_____
_____

What is the name of your family member who was wounded in service?

_____

What is that person's relation to you (is it your dad, mom, brother, sister, or other relative)?

_____

What branch of the military does he or she serve in?

_____

What is your service member's job?

_____

What makes your service member special?

There are lots of reasons to be proud of this person you love.

Find the words in the puzzle that describe some of the qualities
that you admire in this person.

```
T  S  A  U  D  P  R  S  M  H
D  E  D  I  C  A  T  E  D  O
A  L  E  R  H  T  V  I  E  N
D  F  W  D  B  R  A  V  E  E
I  L  O  P  K  I  N  S  K  S
L  E  F  J  C  O  Q  U  I  T
O  S  Y  B  S  T  R  O  N  G
Y  S  G  X  P  I  O  R  D  T
A  T  Y  V  F  C  S  L  H  O
L  C  O  N  F  I  D  E  N  T
```

WORDS:

- BRAVE
- CONFIDENT
- STRONG
- HONEST
- KIND
- LOYAL
- DEDICATED
- PATRIOTIC
- SELFLESS

Your wounded warrior is a hero for his or her qualities and for making the world
a safer place. By serving the country, your loved one puts the needs of other
people before his or her own and makes personal sacrifices for the sake of others.

Your Wounded Warrior

Draw or paste a picture of your hero below.

I am most proud of this person because:

....

....

....

Special Memories

You probably have some special memories about times before your family member deployed.

You can write about those times here.

A happy memory

....
....

Something he or she taught me

....
....

Great advice he or she gave me

....
....

A trip or adventure we shared

....
....

THE MILITARY FAMILY TEAM

Each person in a military family is very important. That's because when you support your service member, you are also supporting your family and the entire country.

Your family makes a lot of sacrifices. For example, in order for your service member to do their job, you must share them with people far away. Also, while your warrior is away, you often miss them, and you do lots of things to hold down the home front.

You and your family need to do things differently during a deployment. You each pitch in and do extra tasks around the house to help keep things in order. Maybe it's your added job to mow the lawn or help take care of a younger sibling. Maybe your sister helps make dinner. Also, you all support your deployed family member when you write letters, call, or send care packages.

When your military hero is away, who takes care of you the most?

....

What are some things this person does that make you happy?

....

....

....

Do you have other relatives or friends who join the team and support you and your family during deployments? If so, you can find some paper and write a thank-you note to let them know that you appreciate them, too.

You Are a HERO, Too!

You are part of your family team,
so don't forget . . . that makes you a hero, too.

I am proud of myself when I:

....

....

....

....

Some sacrifices that I make by
being part of a military family are:

....

....

....

....

I support my family when
I do things like:

....

....

....

I am proud to be in a
military family because:

....

....

....

Bravery

If someone is afraid to do something and then does it anyway, that means they are being brave. Bravery is another word for courage. Service members and their families are especially good at being brave.

People show bravery in many different ways.

Service members show bravery when they leave home to serve our country. It also takes bravery for you and your family members who stay at home to have to say good-bye when your warrior is deployed.

It takes bravery to defend people and to stick up for your beliefs. Military families defend freedom and other values. Maybe you stood up for someone who was bullied or picked on.

It takes bravery to face changes, and military families can have lots of these. You might move to new places, make new friends, change your family routines during deployments, and more. You have lots of practice at being brave through changes.

It takes bravery to ask for help when you need it. It even takes bravery to think and talk about your feelings. So when you feel scared or sad—and even when you cry or get upset—you are still being brave.

You can probably think of ways that you and your family are brave.

Write about one example here.

....

....

....

....

Remember, bravery is a great quality. It's also a really helpful tool to use as you adjust to the changes that happen when someone in your family is wounded.

Wounds from Service

Things to Know about Your Warrior's Wounds,
Medical Care, and Recovery

A service member you love has returned home with an injury. Whether in combat, during deployment, or in training, he or she was hurt while serving our country.

Wounds can be seen or invisible.

Injuries that hurt service members can show on the outside of the body. Just like you can see when people have cuts or bruises, you can see when service members have burns or amputations.

Other times, service members can have wounds that do not show on the outside. Even though you can't see these wounds, they hurt the body on the inside. These wounds are sometimes called "invisible." It's like when you get the flu or a stomachache and you can't see the hurt, but it's very real. When service members hurt their brains or have post-traumatic stress, they may look the same as they did when they were deployed, but these wounds may change the way they feel, talk, or act.

Some wounded people go to the hospital and some don't—but they all need care.

Some service members who are injured severely need to be in the hospital for a while.

Other people who are wounded do not go to the hospital. Instead, they go home and get care from doctors, therapists, or counselors to help them heal.

Healing from wounds takes time . . . but it happens!

Your wounded warrior will get good care from doctors and other health care workers to help them get better. They will also help themselves heal by being brave, strong, and hardworking. Finally, your love and patience will help your wounded warrior feel better, too.

Post-Traumatic Stress

Service members can have experiences or see things that are very scary. These experiences can be so upsetting that they can't stop thinking about them. The feelings are so painful that these service members become wounded by their memories. This is called post-traumatic stress (sometimes called PTSD). Sometimes PTSD makes wounded warriors act differently.

People with PTSD sometimes go to the hospital, but sometimes they don't. Either way, PTSD causes them pain and challenges.

People with PTSD might have nightmares about the upsetting things they saw. This can be hard for them because it means that now they don't get as much sleep as they need. When people are tired, they can get cranky or upset more easily than when they are well-rested.

Giving your wounded warrior time and space to rest when he or she is tired can be very helpful.

In addition to nightmares, wounded warriors may think about these painful memories during the day. These thoughts play like movies in their heads and make wounded warriors feel like they are right back in the scary place. Warriors also may see, smell, or hear things that remind them of their bad experiences. These reminders (called "triggers") can make them very upset. Because of these triggers, people with PTSD might not want to go out and do some things that they used to enjoy. That's because they want to avoid triggers that will make them feel upset.

Be understanding. Think of a really scary movie. Now imagine if your brain made you think of the movie all the time—even when you didn't want to. That's a bit how it can feel when your wounded warrior has these daytime thoughts. Even though he or she knows that these thoughts aren't real life, it can still feel scary.

Come Back Later!

Often, people with PTSD can get quiet and need time alone. These warriors had really hard experiences, and they can get quiet when they are working to find ways to feel calm inside. Sometimes it may be hard for them to show their love. That's because of the PTSD. As they heal, it will become easier for them.

Sometimes it might feel like your wounded warrior is ignoring you. It's OK to miss them, but don't take it personally. He or she is acting distant because of the injury. It's important to know that your warrior still loves you.

Some things can make people with PTSD nervous. Everyday things—such as driving a car on a crowded street, doors slamming, or thunder—can feel stressful to them and make them upset. When they are in loud or busy places, like stores, restaurants, or parties, they might want to leave to avoid feeling upset.

When your wounded warrior gets jumpy, it's because he or she is remembering a time or place where there were bad things happening.

People with PTSD can also act moody. Sometimes they might seem angry and really tense. Other times they appear sad. When they act like this, it's not because of you or anything you did. It's because they may be thinking about close friends who died or other upsetting things that happened while they were deployed.

Try to remember that over time, your wounded warrior will feel better and act calmer.

If your warrior has PTSD, it's good to know that:

- You are not alone. A lot of service members return from deployment with these same challenges, and many families share your experiences.
- People who are strong and brave can have PTSD.
- There are ways they can heal. Therapy can help people with PTSD. Over time, your wounded warrior can learn how to feel better on the inside and act calmer on the outside.

Brain Injury

A traumatic brain injury (TBI for short) is an injury to a person's brain. This can happen when someone gets hit or shaken by a blast or fall. When someone has an injury to the brain, you can't see the damage. This is another kind of invisible wound.

When people have brain injuries, they may go to the hospital for a while. The brain is a very complicated part of the body, and doctors will work to help it heal. However, there are some people who hurt their brains in smaller ways and they might not need to go to the hospital.

TBIs can make people act differently from before they were hurt. Some people will change a lot from a brain injury and others will change in smaller ways.

How people change depends on what parts of their brains were hurt. This is because it's the brain's job to tell the body what to do and when to do it. Each part of the brain is in charge of a different area of the body or a different type of job. Depending on where someone's brain was hurt, they may think, act, move, or talk differently from before.

People with a TBI may get tired easily, sleep a lot, or have a hard time paying attention to things. They might get upset more often or get bad headaches. Sometimes they may forget how to do things that they used to do all the time.

Your wounded warrior will act differently because his or her brain has been changed by the injury. But brains are pretty smart, and there will be ways that it will get better. It may take a long time. Your warrior will work hard with doctors, therapists, and counselors to learn new ways to do things. If there are things that your warrior cannot do anymore, he or she can learn how to feel OK anyway.

Some people with a brain injury or post-traumatic stress have a very hard time concentrating.

Some people get overloaded. That's because they have lots of thoughts and ideas swirling inside their heads all at once. They are also aware of all of the different sounds and sights around them. All of these distractions can make it hard for them to focus on one thing at a time. This might also make them frustrated when too much is going on all at once.

Pretend you are in class and the teacher is giving a math lesson. All of a sudden, someone brings a TV into the room and turns on your favorite show. Then your best friend walks into the room to play with you, a radio starts to play a great song, AND it starts to snow outside. Just then, your teacher asks you to answer a math question.

Wow! You probably forgot to pay attention to her while so many other things were going on, right? Now, the whole class is looking at you and waiting for you to answer the teacher.

Now you can imagine how it might feel to your wounded warrior who feels overloaded and gets distracted easily.

$26+34=?$

$3 \times ?=12$

To do:
1.
2.
3.
4.

Amputations

Service members can get hurt in explosions and lose parts of their legs, arms, or other parts of their bodies.

When people have these injuries, they need to be in a hospital—sometimes for a long time. While they are there, they have surgery and other kinds of care to keep their wounds clean and fix their bones. They may also get skin grafts. That's when doctors take healthy skin from part of a patient's body to cover the places that were wounded.

After some healing time, people with amputations may want to have a new arm, leg, or other body part made to replace the ones they lost. These are called "prosthetic limbs." Some look a bit like robot legs or arms. Others look a lot like regular limbs. Either way, they are made by some very skilled doctors, engineers, and artists to help people with amputations.

Once people get prosthetic limbs, they need to learn how to use them. These warriors spend a lot of time working with doctors and therapists to build their muscles and strength. It's really hard work. While they are getting stronger, they will get tired from all their exercise. They may also get frustrated. Think about how you might feel if you needed to relearn how to walk or do other activities.

People often have several different prosthetic limbs—one for everyday use, one that lets them jog or swim, or others that let them do other things. They can also have a wheelchair for when they need a rest from using their prosthetic leg.

Over time, your wounded warrior will learn how to use the new limb or adjust to not having one. This is a big change, so your family member might do some things differently or more slowly than before. Eventually, he or she will learn to move around and find new ways to do things.

Prosthetic limbs allow people to do lots of activities.

Wounded warriors with amputations can use specially designed limbs to do lots of different activities.

Here, match the prosthetic limb with the activity it's used for.
If you haven't seen all of these prosthetics, you can ask an adult, doctor, or nurse for help.

swimming   skiing   running   basketball   downtime

Now, use your imagination to design a prosthetic limb and draw it here.
Your imaginary leg or arm can look however you'd like, and it can
allow wounded warriors to do anything you imagine—even fly.

Burns

In combat and training areas there are often explosions. Service members who are close enough to the heat may get burned on their hands, fingers, faces, or other parts of their bodies.

These wounded warriors will go to the hospital and may spend some time in a room where they can't have young visitors. Even when they can finally have visitors, warriors usually need to spend most of their time resting.

In the hospital, doctors work hard to fix wounded warriors' burned skin. To do this, doctors take healthy skin from one area of a patient's body and use it to fix the area that was burned. That's called "skin grafting." The doctors also help keep the service members' injuries clean so they won't get infections. To do that, doctors cover the burns with bandages and sometimes do operations. Health care workers also help patients do special exercises that will help them be able to move the parts of their bodies that were burned.

When burns heal, they create scars. Scars can look scary or strange at first, but people get used to them.

Even after people with burns leave the hospital, they'll still have more healing to do.

Even though your wounded warrior's body heals, it may still hurt sometimes.

- When your warrior is outside in the sun or in places that are too warm or too cold, it can hurt their skin.

- Even after operations and exercise, that person still might not be able to bend their arms or legs, or move in ways that were easy before.

- His or her skin probably feels hard where it was burned, like leather. You can touch your loved one, but it's smart to find out which places still hurt so you can avoid touching there.

- Your warrior's skin might itch a lot of the time. This can make him or her grouchy. Imagine if you had mosquito bites that itched and were sore all over your body, but that you couldn't scratch them. Wouldn't that make you frustrated?

People with burns and other injuries might need
to be in the hospital for a while.

Sometimes wounded warriors must be in the hospital for many weeks
or even months. It can be nice to visit your wounded warrior, but
on some days, hospitals might get boring for you.

Here's a maze you can do while you are sitting around. It will remind
you of how valuable your family's service is to our country.

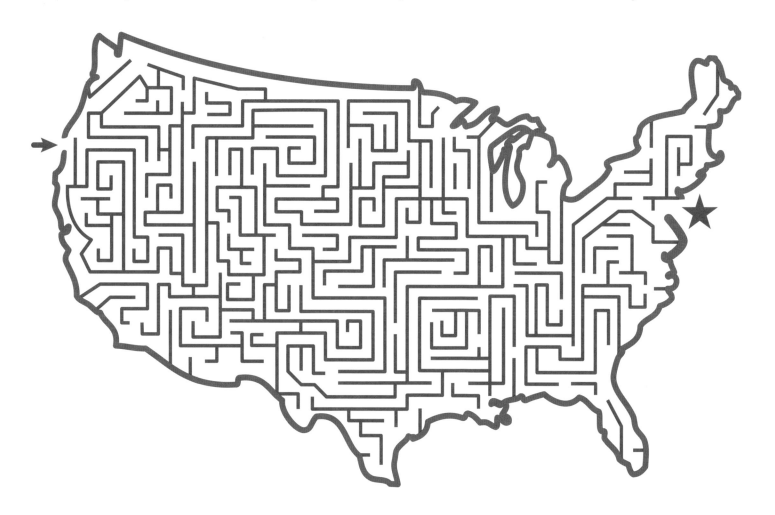

More about Wounds

Your wounded warrior may have other injuries that haven't been explained in this book—like broken bones, wounds to the eyes or ears, or illnesses inside his or her body. Also, your family member may have more than one injury at the same time.

Here are some other things to know about wounded warriors . . . and some things you can do to help.

Even if wounded warriors can do many things that they used to, they may need to find new ways to do them now. That's because their bodies have changed.

If your warrior's wounds prevent him or her from doing some activities with you, you can find new things that you can enjoy doing together. Be creative and remember that no matter what you are doing, it can be nice just to share time with this person you love.

You can be helpful by keeping things off the floor and cleaning up. That will help your warrior move around more safely if he or she has a wheelchair or difficulty moving.

Wounded warriors might get tired doing some activities, so it's smart for them to take a break or rest.

It takes a lot of energy for your warrior's body and brain to heal. It may be upsetting when that person can't spend time doing things with you because he or she is resting. Your loved one is probably just as disappointed as you are. At those times, you can remember that when your warrior rests, it helps him or her to heal and get better.

You can also help out during rest time by keeping things quiet around the house—like talking in a quiet voice, keeping the TV volume low, and not slamming doors.

If warriors have burns or amputations, their bodies may feel sore sometimes. When people feel pain, they might get grouchy or angry. That's normal. People with PTSD or a TBI can also act very tense and even blow up at the people around them. That's because of their wounds and not because of something you did.

When your wounded warrior acts upset, you should remember that it's not your fault and he or she doesn't mean to make you feel bad. Your loved one is really just frustrated about the changes in their life.

While your family member is acting really angry, the best thing to do is to walk away and give that person space. Once they calm down, you can tell them (or another adult) how you feel. For example, you can say that they made you feel bad or scared.

People take medicine to help when they feel pain from injuries. Unfortunately, some medicines make them even more tired. Medicine can also make people act in different ways; for example, they might become forgetful.

If your wounded warrior can't remember things, you should know that it's not because those things aren't important to him or her. It's because of the wound or medicine. Maybe you can help by making a to-do list, reminding him or her about important things, or just by being patient.

 Your wounded warrior may have a brain or body that works differently than it used to, but he or she still loves you just as much as before.

How Do YOU Feel?

People have all sorts of different feelings
when someone they love is wounded in service.

It is important to know that:

Whatever you are feeling is OK.

and

You might have a bunch of different feelings.

and

You might not be sure exactly what you are feeling,
but you might want to cry, yell, sleep, sit quietly,
or run around, and that's OK, too.

and

Your feelings will change—sometimes quickly
and sometimes not so quickly.

Some Common Feelings

There are lots of military families and lots of kids who
have family members who have been hurt.

We asked a bunch of these kids how they felt when their family member
was wounded. We learned that everyone feels different.
Here is what they had to say.

" I kept feeling **LEFT OUT**.
My parents are busy, and it feels like I never
get any time with them. When I told my parents how
I felt, they came up with a great idea. We created a
special code word for me to say when I really want to
spend time with them. Now I don't have to think
of the right thing to say. I can just say
our code word. "

If you feel like this, you
and your family can
create your own code
word and write it here:

....

"I feel sick a lot of the
time. I get stomachaches and
headaches and feel **HURT**
in different places
on my body. "

When someone you love has a bad
injury, it can make your heart hurt—
and it can make your body hurt,
too. It's normal for your body to
react when you are upset. If you feel
like you hurt, tell an adult about it.

Sometimes people stare at my dad or make fun of the way he walks or acts. I used to get **EMBARRASSED**. Now I just tell them that he got hurt serving our country and doing work that keeps us all safe. When I explain it this way to kids at school or people who stare, I feel proud instead of upset!

People sometimes stare when they see things that are unfamiliar to them like scars, burns, and amputations. People also might stare when someone acts differently because of a TBI or PTSD.

If you want, you can ask someone in your family to sit down with you and write down what you can say to people who stare or who don't understand.

....

....

....

I get **MAD** sometimes. Everyone in my family is so busy that I don't get to do all the things that I like to do. Also, my parents don't always come to watch my games or pick me up from school.

Life can be a lot busier when someone in a family is injured. Time has to be made for trips to the hospital, to the doctor, or for other things related to their needs.

It's OK to be mad. One smart kid said that when he felt mad, he tried to remember that he was mad at the wound and the accident, not at his family or himself.

" I'm staying with my grandparents for a while because my mom said she needed to be with my brother at the hospital. I miss them both and feel **SAD**. "

It can be hard on everyone when someone from the family is in the hospital. If your parents need to go away for a little while, it's important to keep remembering that they love you as much as always!

" There's more yelling and other upsetting stuff in my house, and I don't like it. It makes me feel **WORRIED**. "

Sometimes when adults are in pain, they try to ease their hurt in unhealthy ways—like by drinking alcohol, yelling at people, or hitting.

It's smart for you to learn healthy ways to heal when you feel upset. You'll find some tools in this book to help you do that. If you are worried about someone in your family, then you should talk to an adult about it.

" My mom has good days and bad days and it's hard to know what kind of day it will be. I get **CONFUSED**. "

Telling your parents how you feel is healthy and can help make everyone feel better.

Fill in the blanks below and then show this page to your parent when they are in a calm mood.

When you ....

I feel ....

Remember, if you are having strong feelings, you are not alone.

Questions

It's also common to feel afraid when lots of things are changing around you and you have questions on your mind.

How long will he be in the hospital?

Why did this happen?

What's it like to visit the hospital?

Will someone else I love get hurt?

Will she get better?

Why is he acting like that?

Why are people in my family fighting?

Could he die?

What will stay the same?

What's going to happen next?

Who will take care of me?

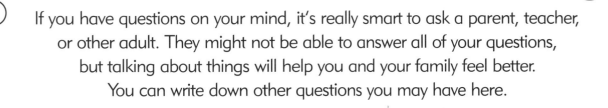

If you have questions on your mind, it's really smart to ask a parent, teacher, or other adult. They might not be able to answer all of your questions, but talking about things will help you and your family feel better. You can write down other questions you may have here.

How do you feel?

The words below are more of the ways people might feel after someone they love has had a bad injury. Have you felt any of these things recently?

Circle any of the words that describe how you have felt.

embarrassed

sad

grumpy

cheated

mad

CONFUSED

ignored

stressed

left alone

tired

WORRIED

quiet

stupid

guilty

sick

OK

SCARED

bored

unsure

jealous

brave

loved

relieved

proud

Are there other words that describe how you have felt? If so, you can write them here.

Look at the words that you circled or wrote down.
Now pick four of those words and write down more about each feeling.

WORD:

When do you feel that way?

_____

_____

What makes you feel that way?

_____

_____

What do you do when you feel that way?

_____

_____

WORD:

When do you feel that way?

_____

_____

What makes you feel that way?

_____

_____

What do you do when you feel that way?

_____

_____

WORD:

Feelings can show on faces. Draw a picture of how you look when you feel like that.

WORD:

Write a poem about what this word means to you.

_____

_____

_____

_____

_____

_____

Draw a Picture

Below, draw a picture that shows how you are feeling today.

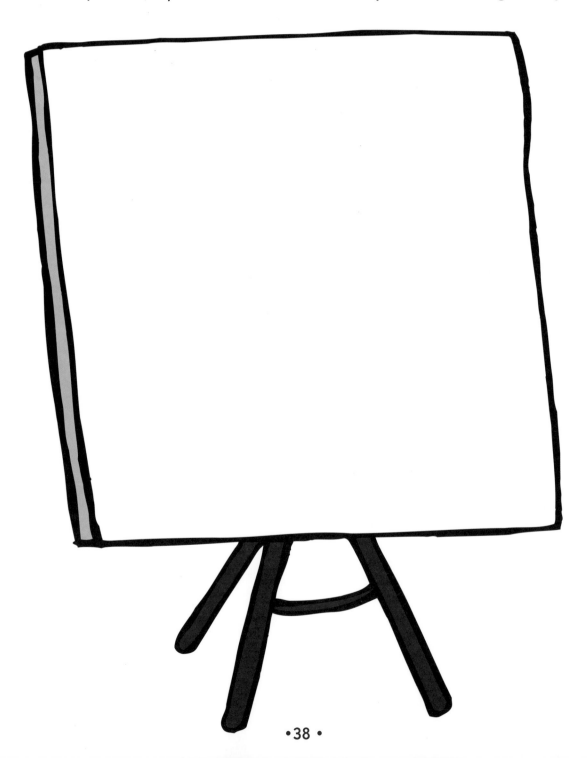

Write It Down

You can use this page to write, scribble, or draw.
Expressing your thoughts and feelings is a great way to get them out!

Thoughts:
1.
2.
3.
4.

Braving the Changes and
MOVING FORWARD
with Your Family

When someone you love comes home from service wounded,
there are lots of challenges for the whole family.

A lot of things are changing and feel different.

When things change, people feel loss. They often miss the way things were.

It's normal for you and your family to be sad about your wounded warrior's injury and to be upset about the other changes that are happening because of it.

But, you will see that you will find ways to grow as you face these challenges together.

Remember, you are brave! It will take some time, but you will all find ways to heal and feel better. You and your family will find new ways to do things. You may even discover that change can be good in some ways that you don't even know yet.

Your family may be different today, tomorrow, and in the future,
but you can still be great.

Change

Change is a natural part of life. It happens all the time.

One place you can see change is in nature. Just think about how a tree looks in the winter and then how it looks in the summer.

People change, too. As people live and have new experiences, they constantly grow and change.

▶ Some changes can feel bad at first, like when you start a new school. In the beginning you don't have any friends and don't know your way around. But before you know it, you've made new friends and can find your way around like a pro.

▶ Some changes happen naturally, like when a tree loses leaves or grows flowers. Others happen because we work on them, like how you get smarter when you study at school.

▶ And some changes happen that we don't expect or because of accidents—like the one that hurt the person you love.

How have you changed?

How tall were you last year? _____ How tall are you today? _____

What is your favorite sport or hobby? _____
As you practice, you get better and better. That's a good change.

You probably enjoy different things today than when you were younger. What was your favorite game or toy when you were five years old? _____
What is it today? _____

Every day you learn new things in school. How much you know keeps changing as you learn more and more!

How many teeth have you lost? _____ When you lose your baby teeth, your smile looks different, and that's a change. Then your smile changes again when your new teeth grow in.

Change can bring wins AND losses.

When things change, it means that they become different.

While your family member was deployed, you grew and changed.

Below, write about some of those changes. You can write about things you learned or accomplished, new friends you made, ways you look different, things that were challenging, or anything else.

Circle the changes that were positive—ones that you were happy about and consider wins. Put a square around ones that feel like losses.

Changes in Your Family

Your wounded warrior had a BIG experience that created a lot of changes in his or her body and life.

What are some of these changes? You can write about changes in how your wounded warrior looks or acts.

....

....

....

....

Your wounded warrior's injury has also caused changes in the lives of other people in your family, too. Maybe your family members need to pay more attention to the person who is hurt. Sometimes they may cry when they feel sad or show other emotions.

Below, you can write about ways that your mom, dad, or other family member is acting differently.

....

....

....

How about you? You're probably acting differently in some ways, too. That's normal. You can write about it here.

What changes have been the hardest for you?

If there are changes that worry or scare you, you can write them here.

You can show this page to an adult and talk about
how you feel about these changes.

The Tale of the Tornado

Once upon a time, there was a family who lived in a beautiful house. One night while they were out to dinner, a tornado came through their town and hit their house.

The tornado picked up the house and whirled it around. When the house finally landed again, the windows were broken, the roof was smashed, the floors were flooded from the rain, and the furniture was scattered all around the house.

When the family came home, they saw that their house had been badly damaged in all sorts of ways. They were all really upset because they liked their house and they couldn't imagine how they'd get it back together and make it look the same as it did before the tornado.

When the sun came out the next day, the family got out their tools and started to fix their house. They all worked together. Sometimes it was hard work and they got tired. Sometimes they asked other people—like friends and relatives—for help. And sometimes, they even had fun while they were working together on their house.

Slowly, they put in new windows, made a new roof, and mopped up the floors. They decided to find new places to put some of the furniture. When they repainted the rooms, they picked some new, bright colors. Then they decided to plant a garden outside.

To rebuild their house, they used patience, teamwork, and bravery. It took them a while, but they did it!

In the end, their house didn't look exactly the same as it did before the tornado, but it looked great and it was still their home.

Write Your Own Story

Now it's your turn to be creative.

Write your own tale about a change that seemed like it would be all
bad at first, but then ended up OK.

You can write a true story about another time when something unexpected happened
that changed life for you. For example, maybe you were upset when you moved to
a new town, but then you made some new friends, joined a sports team,
and many things turned out fine.

Or you can make up a story about someone who faced a change that brought
on some hard challenges—but also some new and good things, too.

Family Helps Family

Even though a lot of things may be changing, one really important thing will always stay the same: your family will always love you and take care of you!

Think about the people in your family. It can be your parents, grandparents, sisters, brothers, aunts, uncles, stepparents, godparents, and even good friends who feel like family.

Write down the names of some of the people who care about you.

Ask for Support

Ask for help or support when you need it. If an adult knows what you need or want, they can help you. Be brave and write it down when you think of something that someone in your family can do to help support you when you are upset.

How can you help family members?

No matter how hard you try, you cannot make the wounds or changes go away. You also can't make someone else's problems disappear. But there are things you can do to support the people you love.

Share a hug

Draw a picture to cheer them up

Tell them you love them

Pitch in by helping around the house

Be quiet if they need rest

Study hard in school

Be patient

Tell them that you are proud of them

You can even ask your family what would be helpful and write down their responses here:

Family Time

As your family adjusts to new ways of doing things,
it's great to do fun activities together.

Draw a picture of something that you and your family could do together that
would make you happy. You can also ask your family members for their ideas.

New Fun-Time Activities

Your warrior might not be able to move in the same ways or do all
of the same activities that you used to do together.

You can find NEW activities to do together with the whole family,
or maybe as special one-on-one time with him or her.

TO DO:
Make a list
of things
you can do
together
now that you
really enjoy

Tomorrow and the Future . . .

A great way to face changes is to be positive and
look ahead by setting GOALS.

A goal is something you want to achieve.

Members of the military accomplish their missions by
setting goals and then working on them.

Think about some things you want to achieve. Write them down on the road signs below.

Your family members each have their own goals. You can also have
family goals, like to heal, take a trip, or spend more time with one another.
You can be a team and plan your family goals together.

Other Ways to
FEEL BETTER

In this chapter, you'll find a bunch of ways
to feel better when you are down.

Here are some ideas to start off the list:

- Play with your pet
- Listen to music
- Take deep breaths
- Learn something new
- Cry
- Go for a walk

- Play ball
- Read a book
- Join a group
- Talk to a counselor
- Be quiet

Remember, everyone feels loss and heals differently.
Some ideas might feel good to you—and others might not.

Turn the page for more ideas about ways to feel better. • • •➤

Say a Prayer.

Some people feel better when they pray. Here you can write down
a prayer or wish you have for your loved one, yourself, or the future.

....

....

....

....

....

....

....

....

Let your friends help.

When you are having a hard time, you might feel
like your friends don't understand you. It's not
that they don't care—maybe they just don't know
what to say or how to act around you.

Even when it seems like they aren't saying or
doing things that help, remember that your
friends care about you.

Think about some of the things you do that make your warrior proud of you.
Then keep doing those things.

What are some things you can do that would make him or her proud?

GOOD CONDUCT

....

....

....

....

....

....

Find a peaceful place.

Lots of people have places that they find calming. Maybe it's the beach, in the woods, or in their bedroom.

When you feel upset, close your eyes and imagine YOUR peaceful place. Think of all the details—how it looks, what it smells like, what sounds you might hear, and how it feels.

Just thinking peaceful thoughts can make you feel better.

Find your community of support.

There's a big world out there filled with people who make up your community. These people can give you support by listening to you, talking with you, giving you advice, or just spending time with you.

The people who can help you may live nearby or far away, they may be old or young. They may already be someone you spend time with . . . or someone you rarely see.

Circle the types of people who you can go to for support.

Teachers Coaches School Counselors

Friends

Neighbors Therapists

Chaplains Parents of Friends

Youth Group Leaders

Doctors or Nurses

Now, write down the names of specific people in your life who fit in these categories. This is your support community.

Helping Hands

Think about the people who lend a hand in your life and fill in the blanks below.

When I feel sad, the person I talk to is:

....

When my parents are busy or having bad days, I can count on these people to spend time and be with me:

....

When I'm in the mood to be quiet, I feel comfortable sitting with this person:

....

When I'm mad or confused, I get good advice from:

....

When I feel scared, I can call people. Here are their names:

....

....

Remember, you have lots of people who can support you. Even though it takes bravery, you should always ask for help when you need it.

Do something nice for someone else.

Sometimes doing something kind for someone else can make YOU feel better.

If you know someone who has a family member who is deployed or wounded, you can give them your support by spending time with them. Even going to a movie or playing ball might be enough to make them feel less lonely.

You can make drawings or send get-well cards to wounded soldiers who are in the hospital and spread some good wishes.

You can also do things for people who are not in military families. For example, you can collect all of the clothes or toys you have outgrown and bring them to a place so they can be shared with people who need them.

Be thankful.

When things are difficult for you and the people you love, it can be hard to remember all of the good things you have. Maybe the person you love is feeling a little better, or you got to take a trip, or you have a new pet.

Below, make a list of things that you are thankful for.

....

....

....

....

....

Play and have fun.

Besides schoolwork and family responsibilities, playing is one of your main jobs as a kid. It's really important that you make time to have fun and do things that you enjoy doing.

Below, make a collage, draw a picture, or paste a photo of you doing things you enjoy.

Your parents want you to be happy and to have fun. In fact, your smiles, laughter, and happiness will make your whole family feel better. So get to it and go have some fun!

OTHER STUFF

Congratulations!

Expressing your feelings can be hard, and it takes a lot of strength. This HEALING HEROES BOOK certificate shows that you are brave and have the skills to face change in your life.

THE HEALING HEROES BOOK

This certificate is awarded to

....

WRITE YOUR NAME HERE

for being brave and for being a true hero!

....

DATE

You have found smart and healthy ways to feel better and move forward during change. You can remember these skills and use them whenever things feel challenging in your life.

The Armed Forces Foundation

The mission of the Armed Forces Foundation (AFF) is to provide comfort and support to members of the United States military and their families.

The Healing Heroes Book

The AFF believes that when our men and women in uniform are called to serve, their families serve, too. When service members are wounded, we know the toll that can take on a family.

We hope this book will be shared far and wide. We believe it will help children make sense of their changed family environments and offer crucial information and suggestions to help them cope.

We hope you and your loved ones have found value from your Healing Heroes Book.

Our Other Programs

Through our other programs, the AFF provides assistance and support including:

- Family Financial Assistance for active duty and veteran families
- School counseling programs in heavily military impacted schools
- Morale trips to provide relief for troops and their families
- "Operation Caring Classroom," aimed at building bridges between military and civilian children in the academic setting
- Lodging costs for loved ones to be close to their service member while they are recuperating in the hospital or rehabilitation setting
- PTSD/TBI outreach to raise awareness and foster the emotional and physical health of service members and their families

The Armed Forces Foundation is eternally grateful for your service and stands at the ready to serve those who have so bravely served us all.
Please feel free to visit our website at www.armedforcesfoundation.org or call the office at 202-547-4713.

Join Watering Can® Press in growing kids with character.

www.wateringcanpress.com

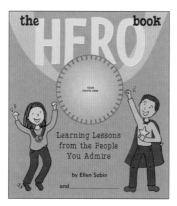
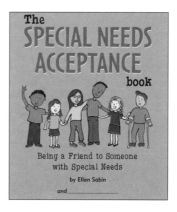
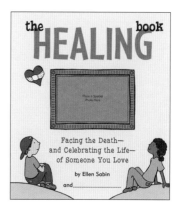

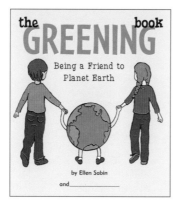
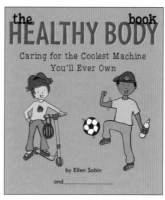
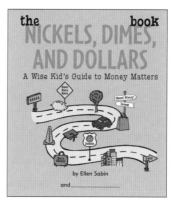

- See other Watering Can® series books.
- Order books for friends/family members or donate copies to an organization serving military families.
- Take advantage of bulk discounts for schools and organizations.
- Learn about customizing our books for corporate and community outreach.
- View the **FREE** Teacher's Guides and Parent's Guides available on our site.

We hope you always remember
that you and your family are
heroes for your service.

Thank You

A special thank you goes to friends and family across the country and to all others who contributed to this recipe collection. I have included all my favorite recipes and I hope you will enjoy them as much as I do.

Edited by Dan Downing and Brett Ortler

Book design by Lora Westberg

Cover design by Jonathan Norberg

10 9 8 7 6 5 4 3 2 1

Copyright 2011 by Theresa Nell Millang
Published by Adventure Publications, Inc.
820 Cleveland St. S
Cambridge, MN 55008
1-800-678-7006
www.adventurepublications.net

ISBN: 978-1-59193-317-5